CW01460280

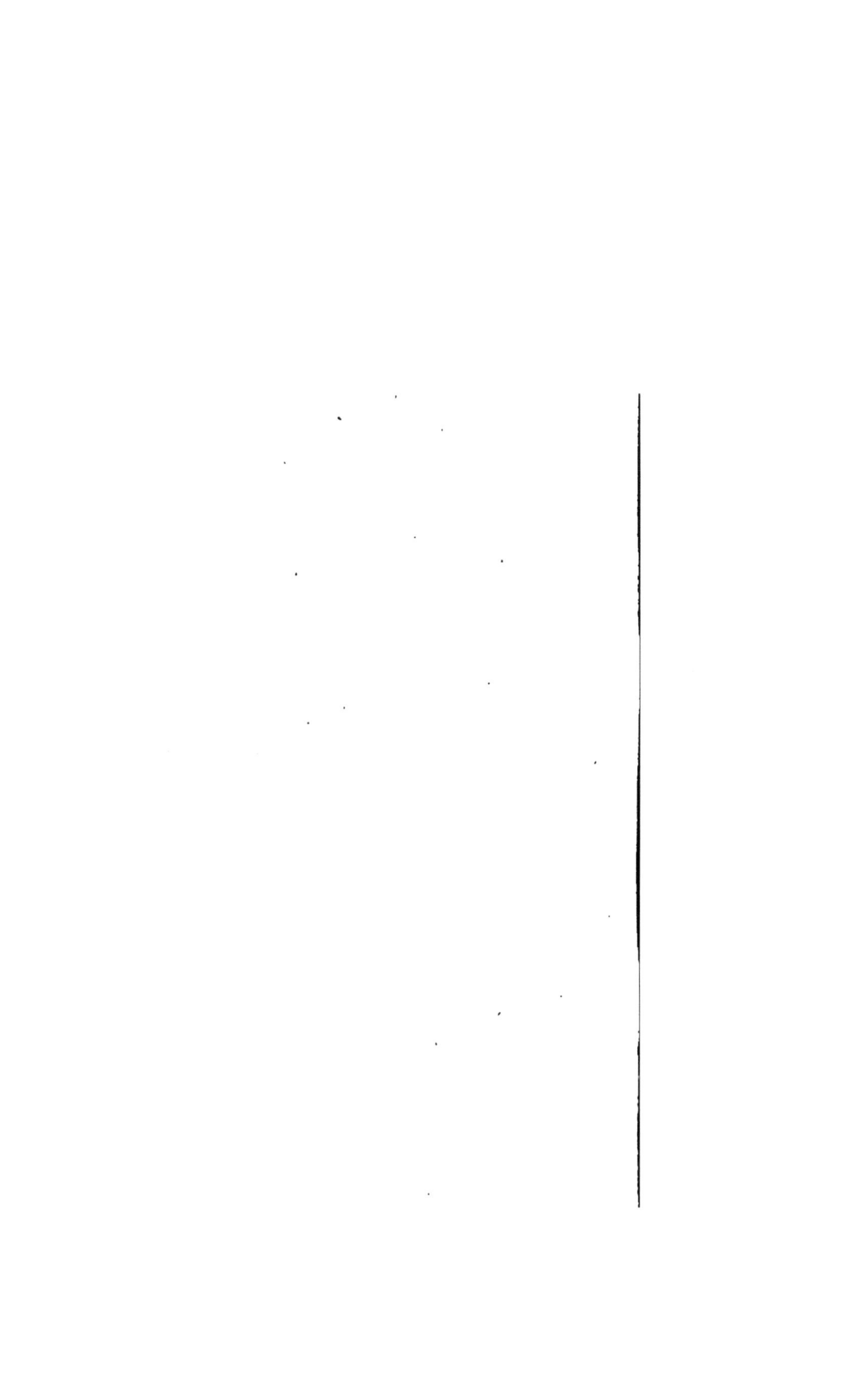

DARWEN

AND

THE COTTON FAMINE.

THIRTY YEARS AGO,

1862—1864.

BY THE

HONORARY SECRETARY OF THE LOCAL RELIEF COMMITTEE.

WITH A BRIEF SUMMARY OF THE OPERATIONS OF THE CENTRAL RELIEF COMMITTEE THROUGHOUT THE COTTON DISTRICT.

J. J. RILEY,
"News" Office, Darwen;
and "Free Press" Office, Rawtenstall.

1893.

CONTENTS.

PREFACE.

Dedicated

TO THE MEMORY OF ONE WHO IN

HER OWN QUIET. UNOBTRUSIVE

MANNER TOOK PART IN THE WORK

HEREIN RECORDED, AND FOR WHOM

SOME HEARTS, IN DARWEN STILL

BEAT WITH GRATITUDE, AND MORE

WITH LOVE.

"Aw make no accawnt o' slotchin' up an' deawn o' this shap, like a foo'. It would sicken a dog, it would for sure. Aw go a fishin' a bit, neaw an' then : an' aw cotter abeawt wi' first one thing an' then another, but it comes to no sense. It's noan like gradely wark. It makes me maunder up an' deawn sometimes like a gonnor wi' a nail in it yed. Aw wish to God yon chaps in Amerikay would play th'up-stroke an' get done wi' their bother, so as foak could start o' wortchin again."

A WIGAN OVERLOOKER.

PREFACE.

THE Author, or compiler, of this small volume, has for many years past purposed its production at some future period ; and feels now that unless the purpose is at once put into execution, it will not be performed at all.

He commends the little book to all who take any interest in its record ; to his friends, the comparatively few survivors of the once large Darwen Committee ; to those who yet remain of the subscribers to, and recipients of the bounty whose story it relates ; and chiefly to the new generation, the descendants, children and grandchildren of those who suffered bitter privations, and manifested the patience, fortitude, and endurance which won for them a Spartan reputation throughout the English speaking world ; and for which they will be esteemed by all honourable men as long as the memory of the Cotton Famine remains.

To the critical reader, who may justly find fault with the loose manner in which the facts are thrown together, he must plead his inexperience in the art and mystery of authorship.

For the interesting facts narrated in the first two parts, the writer is chiefly indebted to a volume entitled " Facts of the Cotton Famine," by the late Dr. John Watts, of Manchester ; himself a member of the Central Committee, and a man to whom many classes of the Lancashire population are for ever indebted, as a pioneer of education, a promoter of Mechanics' Institutions, and other agencies for the instruction both of the young, and those of older growth. To that work he begs to refer such readers as may wish for further information on the subject.

For the facts of the last part, to which indeed the others are but intended as an introduction, the writer is his own authority, having gleaned them from personal recollections, or from his manuscripts of the time, including the minute book of the Darwen Committee still in his possession.

He merely adds that the production has been a labour of love, as was the work of which it tells the story, not to himself alone, but to all those who took part in it.

S. A. N.

September, 1892.

I.

INTRODUCTION.

PRIOR to the year 1741, A.D., the art of making clothing and other articles from raw cotton was truly a manufacture; all such work was done by hand, machinery being non-existent. About that time John Whyatt, of Birmingham, invented a machine to spin a number of threads at once, instead of the spinning wheel which produced only one thread at a time; and John Kay, of Bury, conceived the idea of the fly-shuttle, to be driven by the picking-peg, instead of thrown from hand to hand by the weaver; a wide loom by the old process requiring two weavers. At this date, and long afterwards, spinners fetched their cotton, and weavers their warp and weft, from the masters' warehouse to their own homes, receiving their wages when they took back the finished work. We are told that at this time a piece of coarse cloth, weighing 24 lbs., occupied a weaver's family about a fortnight, the price for weaving was eighteen shillings, for spinning the weft nine shillings, and for preparing the cotton eight shillings, a total

of thirty-five shillings for work alone, exclusive of warp
spinning. Compare this with the price of a piece of 24 lbs.
twill at the present day.

In the year 1781 the total amount of cotton imported into
Britain was equal to 13,000 bales of 400 lbs. each, or very
little more than one day's consumption at the present time.

The machines then or soon afterwards invented, though
they may be termed almost barbarous in comparison with
the nearly perfect automata now in vogue, caused such an
increased consumption of cotton, that by 1800, A.D., it
had reached 129,000 bales of 400 lbs. each; a ten-fold
quantity in the course of twenty years. The work produced
by the spinning frames was also very superior to the old
hand-spun yarns, and cotton warps were substituted for the
linen which had hitherto been used.

The progress of the cotton trade might have been even more
rapid than it afterwards became, but for the burdens placed
upon it by Parliament, which levied a duty on raw cotton in
1795, and continued it till 1845, with no fewer than fourteen
changes in the interval. There was also a duty of sixpence
per square yard on printed calicoes, afterwards reduced to
threepence, and totally abrogated in 1831. Old Darreners,
two generations ago, could tell tales of tricks played on
excisemen when ostensibly engaged in charging the duty.

In those days, as in these, periods of good and bad trade alternated, and the workpeople, ignorant of the mere rudiments of political economy—as indeed were most of their employers—and unacquainted with the great advantages of labour-saving machinery, attributed to the inventions of Hargreaves, Arkwright, Crompton, Kay and others, the sufferings which they were compelled to endure from the scarcity of work and high price of food, and sought their revenge by the destruction of machinery, and the burning of such mills as they found unprotected; while those who ought to have known better looked quietly on.

In the year 1812 evidence was laid before the House of Commons, on the state of trade, and fearful condition of the cotton operatives. Wheat was one hundred and twenty-two shillings and eightpence per quarter; bread, or even potatoes, were out of reach of the people, whose condition was most pitiable. Bad harvests and exorbitant war taxes had largely caused the distress; but the operatives laid it chiefly upon the improvements in machinery, and concluded that if all machines worked by other than hand power were destroyed, there would be more work and wages for them. There was a food riot in Manchester in April, 1812; quelled by the authorities compelling a reduction in the price of potatoes from fourteen shillings or more, to eight shillings

per load.   The soldiers were called out to keep the peace,
and the farmers refused to bring their produce to market
till the magistrates promised protection, one cart-load of
meal having been carried away.   In the same month the
mob attempted the destruction of a mill at Middleton, which
had been erected for weaving by steam.   The owners,
however, forewarned, defended the building; and on its
being attacked and the windows broken, fired upon the
crowd, killing three and wounding many.   Next day the
mob, armed, returned to the charge, but the mill was now
defended by soldiers; so the rioters turned away to the
master's house, and set it on fire.   Later in the same month
a mob attempted the destruction of power-looms at West
Houghton.   Soldiers were sent from Bolton, who, finding
all quiet, returned; after which the rioters set fire to a
factory and destroyed it.   For these and other riots a
fearful retribution was exacted, as we are told that at the
next assizes more than twenty persons were sent to the
gallows, some of whom were very young.

After this came the Corn Law of 1815, keeping up the
price of bread, till its repeal, after much agitation, in 1846.
In the years 1825-26, there was terrible destitution throughout the country.   Fifty-eight banks failed.   In Lancashire
the people, still erring as to the true causes of distress, again

wreaked their vengeance on machinery. They damaged a factory at Accrington, and ill-used the manager when he expostulated with them. Five days later at the same town they destroyed sixty looms, and damaged the steam engine. At Rough Hey they smashed twenty looms, and eighty more at White Ash. The work of destruction was continued at Blackburn till the arrival of the soldiers, who killed one man and wounded others. The first Mr. Eccles Shorrock, of Darwen, gave evidence against the rioters, at the Lancaster Assizes, the following August.

One day in April, 1826, manufacturers returning from Manchester by coach were received in Blackburn with showers of stones. The military saved the mills of Messrs. Turner, at Helmshore ; but two hundred and twenty looms were destroyed at Rawtenstall and Edenfield ; while the lives of four men and one woman were lost in a contest with the soldiery at Ramsbottom. Seventy-four looms were smashed at Summerseat, and more than fifty at Bacup. Two lots of looms were broken up at Darwen ; thirty-six belonging to Mr. James Grime, and sixteen to Messrs. Carr & Co.

At a large meeting of the unemployed in St. George's Fields, Manchester, the people were urged to continue the destruction of power-looms as the cause of the distress ; but

a more sensible working-man, named Hodgins, told them
that all they would get by it would be death from the
soldiers, while the system against which they had arisen
would remain. A large subscription was made, bacon and
meal were freely distributed, and the people, having food,
were pacified.

Again in 1829 a panic prevailed; less employment and
lower wages caused discontent, and the rage against
machinery once more obtained. The windows in a factory
at Macclesfield were all broken. At Rochdale a number of
weavers on strike went round and took away the shuttles of
those at work, an effectual way of stopping them; and next
day the machinery in two factories was destroyed. Sixteen
of the rioters were arrested, and six were killed by the
soldiers in charge, on an attempt to rescue the prisoners.
On the 3rd May, at Manchester, a mob broke into a mill in
Mather Street, turned out the hands, cut to pieces the warps,
broke the reeds, &c., and threw the cloth into the street.
In Pollard Street they destroyed one hundred and thirty-
eight looms; then returning to the first mill, smashed
fifty-three more looms, and threw warps and weft into the
canal. In Ludgate Street they destroyed looms, and set fire
to the mill. The arrival of soldiers stopped further havoc;
but for two more days provision shops were sacked, and
food and money forcibly taken from many houses.

This seems to have been almost the last of the riots in Lancashire against machinery as such; though there have been more in other parts of the country, where ignorance still prevailed; as in Coventry, in 1835, when steam power was first applied to ribbon weaving.

Again, in 1842, occurred in Lancashire what were called the plug riots, which the present writer well remembers; but these were political, and not trade riots. Bodies of work-people went from mill to mill, and from town to town, knocking the boiler plugs out, and thus forcibly stopping the machinery; the Chartists having resolved that all work should cease, till Government yielded the seven points of the Charter.

Many readers will remember the disturbances at Black-burn and Darwen in 1878, which, though a mere flash in the pan when compared with former riots, brought suffering to some, and a long term of imprisonment to two or three convicted of arson.

II

THE CENTRAL COMMITTEE.

FROM 1801 to 1861, the total per centage of decennial increase in the population of England and Wales was 87, while in Lancashire it was 142; and in the latter case the total increase was from 673,486 in 1801, to 2,429,440 in 1861, or nearly 300 per cent; in 1891 the population was 3,926,798. In 1815 the annual value of real property in England and Wales was £51,790,879; in 1861, £112,802,749. In Lancashire alone, the respective figures are: 1801, £3,087,774; 1861, £11,289,315. In 1830 the number of yards of cloth woven was 914,773,563; in 1860, 4,431,281,728 yards; an increase of 384 per cent. in thirty years. The consumption of cotton in 1840 was 528,142,743 lbs.; in 1860, 1,040,000,000; nearly 100 per cent. in twenty years. In 1861 the number of persons employed in textile manufactures in Lancashire was 192,333 males, and 233,789 females, a total of 426,122.

On the eve of the American Civil War, few persons in this country believed that the North and South would fight, but thought that the South was blustering for the extension of slavery, and that the North was bent upon the assertion of its supremacy. And even when the conflict had commenced, and Fort Sumter was captured, the general opinion was that the struggle would be of short duration; that some "ninety days" would see the end of it. The result proved it to be a life or death struggle; that the North must be completely overpowered, or the South subjugated.

Our object, however, is not to describe the course of the American War, deeply as we were interested in it, but its effect upon the cotton operatives of Lancashire, and on those dependent upon them.

On New Year's Day, 1861, there was a four months' supply of cotton in Liverpool, and for the first three months of that year the imports were on the usual scale, with a five months' stock of goods in the Merchants' hands; before these were consumed it was anticipated that the Southern rebellion would be suppressed, the cotton in the States released, and the trade have resumed its usual course. For the greater part of the year the market was dull, and not till its close did prices begin to move upwards, and speculators in cotton become more than usually active. The Federals had declared a blockade of the Southern ports; and the Confederates, believing that in England cotton was king, thought the Old Country could not do without it, and must take their side in order to procure its release.

Now began a state of affairs in Lancashire which must redound to the everlasting honour of the working classes of the county, and of the whole cotton district. Never in the history of the world did any class bear such a calamity as overwhelmed this district, with the exemplary fortitude, patience and forbearance, manifested by the whole population, or almost unanimously. For, though some few wrong-headed individuals advocated the interference of our Government betwixt the belligerents, or, at least, the recognition of the Confederate rulers, which would have been equivalent to a declaration of war against the North, their numbers were so small, and their influence so slight, that their action showed but as a foil to add more lustre to the conduct of the mass of their fellows, who bore without a murmur, and with unexampled patience, the pangs of poverty, hunger and extreme destitution, not only in their own persons, but, which was the source of far intenser suffering to many of them, the pinched, wan looks of their children, pining for food and fire, and the suffering of parents, and other aged relatives, from the same cause.

In October, 1861, mills began to run short time, or to close ; and there were about three thousand additional applicants for poor relief in the twenty-eight Unions of the district. In November there were seven thousand more, and another seven thousand in December; altogether about 25 per cent. more than in the previous January. January, 1862, added another sixteen thousand to the applicants for poor relief; but this forms no real standard of the actual distress, for, naturally, these applicants were of the lowest class. Workpeople of a higher grade, or of frugal habits, had some resources on which to fall back, and it would be months with many of them before these were exhausted, and the pinch of real want felt; and the event proved that there were many, probably thousands, who would have died rather than ask for such relief, even under the direst necessity. The month of February added nearly nine thousand more extra cases, which now amounted to 105 per cent. over the average of twelve months before; while in some Unions these figures were largely exceeded. At Ashton the excess of pauperism was 213 per cent.; Stockport, 263; Blackburn, 270; Glossop, 300; and Preston, 320 over the usual amount.

During this period aid outside that of the Poor-law began to be sought, and benevolent persons started soup kitchens, and relief funds, for those places which were suffering the most. In Ashton there were 3,197, in Stockport 8,588, and in Preston 9,488 persons utterly without food, who positively refused to go to the Guardians.   How could these be left to starvation, or driven to despair !

Organizations arose when the necessity was urgent.   By April committees were formed at Ashton, Stockport, Preston and Blackburn.   In May, Oldham and Prestwich followed. And while very large numbers were dependent on the Relief Committees, the average pauperism of the cotton districts was 131 per cent. in excess of 1861.   The newspapers denounced the apathy of manufacturers, but their editors were often ignorant of the assistance which was being quietly given ; though it must be admitted that some few rich men were callous to the rightful claims upon them, and either refused their aid, or gave in so niggard a spirit that their help was of little value.   Yet these were the exceptions to the rule, and their stingy hardheartedness made more conspic-uous the generosity of those who devised liberal things, many of whom gave even of their poverty to their neighbours poorer than themselves.

By the month of July, 1862, we are told that " the distress increased like a flood "; and in August, " the flood had become a deluge, at which the stoutest heart might stand appalled." The increase of pauperism was almost incredible. In Preston it was more than 1,000 per cent. in excess of ordinary relief.   More than 27 per cent. of the population were in want of the commonest necessaries of life, and, though willing and anxious to work, knew not how to earn a meal. Many of the shopkeepers were reduced to comparative destitution. The number of local Relief Committees by August was seventeen, and a Central Executive Committee had been appointed at Manchester in May. Before the end of the year the applicants for relief were increasing by thousands a day.

By this time American cotton was becoming a scarce article, and thousands of unemployed were only too glad when they got the chance of working at " Surats "—the much-decried material of better times. In Manchester now a local Relief Committee was required, not so much for cotton workers, but for the thousands in other branches dependent upon the trade. Clerks, warehousemen, porters, small tradesmen, and even owners of cottage property, who could draw no rents, but had many outgoings for which they were unable to provide. As winter approaches the authorities are almost at their wits' end for the wherewithal to supply the hundreds of thousands in want of food, and utterly unprepared for the hardships of the season ; much of the clothing and other necessaries having been pledged or sold for anything that it would fetch. In November another forty-four thousand became recipients of relief from the Guardians,

and a like number were added to those dependent upon
Relief Committees. In this month were relieved by these
two bodies of distributors, in the Unions of

Blackburn, 31·8 per cent. of the whole population.

Glossop, 35·9 per cent.

Ashton-under-Lyne, 41·8 per cent.

Preston, 47·5 per cent.

In the last case, all but one-half of the people of the district.
Throughout Lancashire nearly half-a-million of industrious,
prosperous people were suddenly, by no fault of their
own, thrown out of employment and reduced to destitution;
and were to be found, as we have already said—and it will
bear repetition—exhibiting a degree of unexampled and
patient endurance, while waiting for a supply of the material
for their labour which was so tardy to come.

To prevent those who were thus driven to receive relief
from the various committees, from sinking into habits which
would lead to subsequent pauperism, various schemes were
devised for their employment in works of utility, and in
education. Thus the men were set to repair the old footpaths in their respective neighbourhoods, or to form new
roads; the women and girls were gathered into sewing
classes; and many learnt there what they ought to have been
taught before, and what was useful to them in after-life, when

all such evil times had passed away. Old and young, of both sexes, were gathered into schools, attendance at which, in most cases, was compulsory, or relief would be withheld. In these schools might sometimes be seen youths with their fathers and grandfathers, learning to read and write in the same class. Old persons, in some cases, learnt to read who were ignorant of the alphabet before. Masters were paid sums varying from fifteen to thirty shillings a week, and were assisted by the most intelligent pupils, who were paid a small sum in addition to their relief allowance. The attendance was during the day, but many of the schools were also open at night for instruction and recreation ; and in some places lectures and concerts were given. Some of the rooms in old mills thus used, were decorated by the operatives with brush and water-colours, and so ornamented as to be fit almost for ballrooms ; the effects of which were cheering and exhilarating to the people. The girls in the sewing schools, brought into contact with refined and educated ladies who superintended and taught them, came under influences, and received softening touches which they could never otherwise have felt ; and many hitherto unaccustomed to domestic occupations, learnt to sew, darn, and make garments ; and in cooking schools were taught to prepare dishes and meals in a way with which many of their mothers were unacquainted.

And the materials worked up in the sewing classes, provided raiment for thousands who would otherwise have been almost naked. These schools lasted two and a half years, and the number of scholars varied from four thousand three hundred and seventy-nine in November, 1862, to more than one hundred and thirty-five thousand in March, 1863; thence diminishing till the end, in June, 1865, when there were still six hundred and forty-eight in attendance.

In Manchester, and other large towns, parties of the unemployed roamed through the streets, singing plaintive ditties, or hymns to the fine old tunes for which Lancashire psalmody is famous. Of one of these tunes, "Warrington," a story is told which we would fain help to rescue from oblivion. It was composed by a Rev. Mr. Harrison, Unitarian minister of Cross Street Chapel, Manchester. " One day an old weaver, who had come down from the hills many miles, knocked at the door, and asked if a gentleman co'de Harrison lived there ? ' Yes.' ' Could aw see him ?' ' Yes.' When the minister came to the door, the old weaver looked hard at him for a minute, then said, ' Are yo th' mon 'at composed that tune co'de Warrington ?' ' Yes,' replied the minister, 'I believe I am.' ' Well,' said the old man, ' gi' me yor hond ! It's a good un.' He then shook hands heartily with him again, and, saying 'Well, good-day to yo,' went his way home again, before the old minister could fairly collect his scattered thoughts."

At the commencement of the period of distress, the Boards of Guardians had enforced the usual labour test; but after a meeting of operatives, in June, 1862, held in Stevenson Square, Manchester, which resolved that "it is unwise and unjust to compel honest working-men to perform that kind of labour which common felons are required to perform," and sent a deputation to the Guardians of Manchester, with the resolutions passed at the meeting, these gentlemen adopted the suggestion made by one of the deputation—as did afterwards the various Relief Committees—and substituted the school for the labour test; the change being most satisfactory and successful, as already described.

At the request of the Central Relief Committee, the Government sent to their assistance a gentleman from the Poor-law Board, Mr. Farnall, who reported that while in May, 1861, there were in the Union of Ashton-under-Lyne, out of a population of one hundred and thirty-five thousand, not quite eleven hundred in receipt of parochial relief, in the same Union there were, in May, 1862, thirty-two thousand eight hundred and eighty-one persons so relieved; and he adds that the poverty is still increasing. The Commissioner, closing his statement, observes that this town illustrates the position of other large towns and localities ; and gives an assurance " to those benevolent persons in England and the Colonies who are now charitably aiding the Lancashire workpeople, that their subscriptions are saving thousands of meritorious operatives and their children, whose spirits are yet unbroken, from the necessity of applying for parochial relief, and are, at the same time, attaching to themselves a class of people whose present conduct is a guarantee of their sterling goodness."

In April, 1862, began a series of letters in the London *Times*, from " A Lancashire Lad," pleading earnestly the cause of the distressed cotton operatives. He also wrote to the Lord Mayor of London, who received, on the 25th April, a deputation of City merchants seeking to interest him, and, through him, the public, in the widespread and increasing distress in the manufacturing districts of Lancashire. His Lordship and the deputation formed themselves into a Provisional Committee for the receipt of contributions, to be forwarded to such Local Committees as should be established in the distressed districts. Thus originated the first general subscription for the cotton operatives ; and the Mansion House Fund, before its close, amounted to the grand total of £528,366 9s. 9d., of which £183,031 2s. 5d. came from the British Colonies and foreign countries.

Four days after the deputation to the Lord Mayor, a meeting was held in Manchester of residents, convened by Mr. Goadsby, the Mayor, at which an opinion was expressed that there was no necessity for other than existing agencies for dealing with the distress, and no action was taken. But those at a distance were more alive to the necessities of the county, and money was already pouring into the Mansion House Fund. In the course of another month the Mayor of Manchester felt constrained to summon another meeting; this time to consider a scheme for loans to the unemployed, it being argued that gifts would pauperise the people. Others reasoned that a burden of debt would destroy all manliness, and that it would be better when the time of trouble was over, that all should start with a free hand. There were still men present who wished to do nothing; but it was at last resolved to adjourn the meeting for a week. Before the lapse of that interval a committee had been formed, composed chiefly of Manchester men; to whom were added afterwards the Mayors and ex-Mayors of all boroughs in the cotton districts.

A number of subscriptions were announced at the adjourned meeting; also that the Rev. E. Walker, of Cheltenham, had made a collection in his church for the same object, amounting to £384; and this gentleman

reported, at the end of October, that a second collection had
been made throughout the town, realising £1,076 1s. 7d.

On the 19th July, a meeting of noblemen and members of Parliament from Lancashire was held in London,
called by the Earl of Derby and Colonel Wilson Patten,
M.P., who died so recently—Lord Winmarleigh—at the
venerable age of ninety, honoured and loved of all. In five
days the subscription inaugurated at this meeting, reached
£17,000, subsequently augmented to £52,000.

At a meeting of the Central Committee, held at Manchester, November 3rd, 1862, Lord Derby in the chair, Mr.
Cobden was present, and advised a bold appeal to the
whole country, declaring that £1,000,000 would be required
to carry the sufferers through the crisis, and the subscriptions hitherto amounted but to £180,000. He suggested
that the labours of the General Committee might be well
employed in increasing the amount of subscriptions. It
had been stated that the loss of wages was now at the rate of
£136,094 per week, representing more than £7,000,000
per annum. The present resources would yield £25,000
per month for five months, being less than 5 per cent. on the
actual loss of wages. He had always foreseen that the
distress and suffering must be cumulative to an extraordinary
degree, because, as poverty increased, the usual means of

relieving it would diminish, ratable property decreasing in value, and much of it becoming unsaleable. The mass of labouring population in the county were now reduced to one dead level, and the poor-rates and voluntary subscriptions were all that was available for their subsistence. The health and strength of the community would suffer, and mental and physical prostration prevail, unless some greater effort at prevention were adopted. The state of matters was totally exceptional—had no parallel in history. The calamity was unprecedented in its suddenness, in the impossibility of effectually dealing with it, or supplying an adequate remedy. It was only the nation at large that could deal with it, and "we must be reminded that a national responsibility rests upon us." He therefore recommended that the General Committee should be made a National Committee.

The Central Executive slowly awakened to the necessity of more active effort. Mr. Cobden's speech roused the General Committee, and, in accordance with his suggestion, a Collecting Committee was appointed at the next meeting; and by the end of January, 1863, in Manchester and Salford, £130,000 had been collected. It was felt that Manchester, not needing help, had a duty to perform to other places, and donations were so freely given, that those who solicited them, accustomed to sneers and excuses on ordinary occasions, were astonished; for they found themselves often thanked for giving the opportunity to subscribe to the fund. The character of the gifts was as remarkable as the amount. Many of the donations were not in one sum, but monthly subscriptions, promised as long as the necessity should last.

In the winter of 1862-3 a Ladies' Committee was formed in Manchester, and a special fund raised to release from pawn the clothes of the destitute operatives, forced to part with them for food; and hundreds of families found themselves thus unexpectedly provided against the cold blasts of winter.

Accusations were made in the *Times*, by leading articles, and by letters from the Rev. Charles Kingsley, against the capitalists and millowners of Lancashire, of neglect of their own duties, and niggardliness in contributing to the relief of their own workpeople; and a large increase in the Poor Rates of Lancashire Unions was declared to be the proper means of meeting the necessities of the case. These charges were copied into other papers, and disseminated throughout the kingdom, retarding the flow of contributions till deputations from the Central Committee had visited many places, and explained the truth of matters. No more was heard of

these animadversions after a meeting of the County of
Lancaster, on the 2nd December, at which Lord Derby
eloquently defended the manufacturers for their conduct
under unexampled difficulties, and " became on that day the
powerful and successful representative of the poor and
helpless." His lordship said, " It is very hard to ascertain
with any certainty what has been done by Lancashire,
because, in the first place, the amount of local subscriptions,
and the amount of public contributions, by themselves give
no fair indication of that which really has been done by
public or private charity. . . . Many have acted with
the most princely munificence, liberality, and generous
feeling, involving an amount of sacrifice of which no persons
out of this county can possibly have the slightest conception."
He then gave extracts from reports confidentially supplied
by Mr. Commissioner Farnall. These extracts, without
giving names, instanced one employer who, at his own cost,
pays five hundred and fifty-five girls eighteenpence weekly,
for attending a sewing class—four hundred and eight men
and boys from fourpence to eightpence a day, according to
age, for attending school, and also pays the school-pence ;
and in addition gives bread, soup, socks, and clogs.
Another master, who has hitherto been paying two days'
wages per week, is now preparing to adopt a similar scheme.

A third, at his own expense, provides fifty or sixty dinners daily for the sick, and has a comfortable soup kitchen fitted up. A fourth firm pay their hands three days' wages, about £500 per week. Other firms pay two days' wages a week. Much private charity exists. One firm has spent £1,400, besides weekly doles of bread. Another provides all old hands with clothing and bedding. The ladies of one village visit and relieve with money, food, or clothing ; or with all if urgently needed. Generally the poor are living rent free. Payment of rent is almost unknown. The receipts of some owners of property are not sufficient to pay the property-tax. The Committee received an application from a small district where was one mill worked by some young men not long in business. The application was refused because there was no local subscription ; but on inquiry being made it was found that the mill had been many months closed, and these young men had maintained the whole of their hands ; they paid one-third of the rates of the district, and were losing £300 a year from unpaid rent of their cottages. This case shows how persons at a distance may be deceived by the apparent want of local subscriptions. Lord Derby continued that he would throw all this out of consideration, and appeal to the reports of the Commissioner himself, to whom much praise was due, and than whom no better authority could be quoted.

To date, the total amount contributed was £540,000. Of this sum £40,000 came from the Colonies, £100,000 from the rest of the kingdom, and £400,000, in round numbers, from the County of Lancaster itself. These figures were sufficient to do away with the imputation that Lancashire at this crisis was not doing its duty; but His Lordship urged that the county should not relax its efforts, for the height of the distress was not yet reached. The state of things called for most active exertions from the whole community, who thus far had responded to the call most nobly. The Queen had sent a donation of £2,000. The first act of the Prince of Wales on attaining his majority was to write from Rome and request that his name should be put down for £1,000. At the other end of the scale, a donation of £1,200 had been received from some thousands of working-men, readers of a periodical called the *British Workman*, including even the brigade of shoe-black boys. All classes had displayed the greatest liberality; the poor in every district had contributed more than their share in proportion to their means. Lord Derby concluded by proposing a resolution to the purport that the working-classes of the district, suffering from an extent of destitution hitherto unknown, had borne it " with a patient submission and resolution entitling them to the warmest sympathy of their

fellow-countrymen." The result of the meeting was a subscription list of £70,000, added thereby to the Relief Fund.

The aid of emigration was also sought to relieve the con-
gestion of the cotton districts ; but though many thousands
of operatives are known thus to have been taken away, there
is no means of ascertaining the actual number.   Agents
came from America to secure what workers they could for
the cotton mills there ; yet, though they would take all
cotton operatives, or men who would enlist in the Federal
armies, they refused to be hampered with families, or those
otherwise dependent on the workers.

The collapse of the cotton trade naturally stimulated the
linen, and woollen and worsted trades ; and other thousands
migrated to Yorkshire and other localities where these trades
flourished.   Altogether, about one-fourth of the cotton
operatives found new homes or occupations for themselves.

As we have seen, the distress and the number of persons
in receipt of relief, culminated in December, 1862, when
there were near half-a-million individuals so relieved.   The
number gradually diminished till August, 1864, when it
stood at 83,063.   At this date a panic arose from a rumour
of negotiations for peace in the States ; and Middling
Orleans fell from thirty-one pence to twenty-three pence half-
penny per lb., and many of those in the trade, who held

stocks, were ruined, and mills closed. Some additional sixty or seventy thousand persons were again thrown out of work, and in November the number of the relieved was 149,923. From this time a regular declension set in, and in May, 1865, the number was 75,784; and in the following month of June, the Honorary Secretary of the committee was able to say that he did not intend to publish any further returns.

Mr. Cobden, at an early stage of relief operations had estimated, that one million sterling would be needed as a national subscription; but the total amount of public contributions, in money and in kind, was £1,773,968. Of this total, cash was distributed by the various committees, £1,661,679, and goods contributed of various kinds, to the value of £111,968. The latter, sent to the Central Committee, consisted of 16,500 barrels of flour; 697 barrels of beef, bacon, &c.; 300 barrels of biscuits; 410 cases of fish; 228 sacks of potatoes, carrots, &c.; 28 chests of tea; 2½ pipes and 108 dozens of wine; 11,519 tons of coal; 893 bales of clothing, blankets, &c.; 225 deer, and many hundreds of pheasants, hares, rabbits, &c.

In addition to these gifts, we know that many contributions were sent to secretaries, and other individual members of Relief Committees, and also to private persons for their own distribution, of money and clothing, and of other articles, of which the Central Committee never heard, and therefore could not acknowledge. These would swell the aggregate to a value that none can correctly estimate. It has been calculated at £200,000, and this is probably below the real sum.

One great gift sent to the Central Committee, stirred the heart of Lancashire, and of the nation, to an unprecedented degree, and excited universal gratitude. It was originated by George Griswold, a merchant of New York, who sent his own ship, bearing his own name, freighted with flour and other provisions; paying all expenses, and sending all across to help the distressed operatives of Lancashire. Probably his noble example stimulated the expression of sympathy by others of his countrymen, who sent supplies of food over the water, to the unwilling idlers on this side. When the "George Griswold" arrived in port, the Custom House officers did not board the vessel, no dock or town dues were exacted, and everybody employed, down to the dock porters and tide waiters, refused payment for their services, and the railway companies carried the freight free of charge. The captain of the vessel was made the guest of the Corporation of Liverpool, and of the Central Relief Committee at Manchester. At a public dinner in this city, an address, enclosed in a morocco case, was presented to Captain Lunt, who, in the course of his reply, said: "The donors of the cargo will be highly gratified with this most cordial welcome. The contributions of the merchants of New York were given solely for their sympathy with your suffering operatives. Stevedores, tugging-boats, shipping masters, all contributed their services. I am happy to publish this, the right good-fellowship of the labouring-classes in so good a cause. On my arrival at the Port of Liverpool, I found the steam companies vieing with each other to tow my ship to port free of charge. . . . My heart warms to each and every one of those volunteers, whose liberality I deem it only right thus publicly to acknowledge. I shall ever cherish the friendly feeling shown to me in Liverpool and Manchester, and shall carry back to my country the noble reception . . . and the good feeling expressed for the United States by many able gentlemen, at different times since my arrival. God grant that . . . England and America may ever extend the hand of good-fellowship to each other."

Subscriptions—chiefly given by British residents—were also received from many other countries. A most interesting contribution at home, was that of the Society of Painters in Water Colours, who requested each member to present one (or more) painting to be exhibited, and afterwards awarded as prizes to subscribers. The exhibition contained three hundred and eighteen pictures, and was the means of adding £1904 16s. 9d. to the Relief Fund. Mr. Ansdell, R.A., gave a fine work, " The Hunted Slave," to the fund, and it realised £696 3s. The readers of the *British Workman*, whose early contribution we have already recorded, and who comprised all classes of artisans and workers, subscribed in all £3,564 10s. 1d. Among the long list of contributories some curious specimens are to be found, of which the following are a few :—

	£	s.	d.
Budding Sympathies	0	7	0
A Marksman's Prizes	0	2	0
Polly (for two weeks)	0	1	0
Dispute at a Bachelors' Club	0	6	6
Vain is the help of Man	0	5	0
Haud Ignarus Mali	0	12	6
A Merry Convivium Germanium	0	12	6
A Lady's Maid	0	5	0
Winnings of a Party at Speculation	0	2	0
A Widow	0	0	1
Odds and Ends Collected at Filey	1	0	0
Six-Seventy	1	0	0
Plain Roast and Boiled	0	4	0
Savings from an Old Smoker's Pipe	0	2	0

£ s. d.

Forty Little Boys, saved from pleasures

    usual on 5th November 7 0 0

A Penny Lecture on Cotton 0 16 8

A Trifle from a Housemaid 0 3 0

and many more might be given. The sympathy thus practically manifested by all classes was universal; never was there such an outpouring of free-will offerings, or such a demonstration of brotherhood from those both near and afar off. Nor was evidence wanting of the truth that

> " The quality of mercy is not strained ;
> It droppeth as the gentle rain from Heaven .
> Upon the place beneath : It is twice bless'd ;
> It blesseth him that gives, and him that takes."

The generous donors were blessed in the enlargement of their own hearts, drawn out in loving sympathy for their unfortunate fellows ; and the recipients were blessed, not only in the relief of their utter extremity, but by the feeling of deepest gratitude elicited ; and in many cases.the softening of hitherto callous hearts, opened by the generous manifestations of loving kindness, to reciprocal tenderness unknown before.

It is remarkable that through the whole of the Cotton Famine, the health of the population was well maintained, notwithstanding the privations experienced, and the crowding

together, in many instances, of families who had before
occupied separate domiciles.   It may be that the greater
frugality and temperance, necessarily enforced, partly accounts
for this.   But, whatever may have been the cause, the fact is
undeniable, that the usual sad effects of destitution and want
did not follow here.   All inquiries instituted by the Central
Committee proved, that the three years of severe suffering in
the cotton districts, passed without increasing the death-rate,
or the normal amount of disease.

In the period about 1832, the average mortality of Manchester for ten years was 35·22 per cent.   Dr. J. P. Kay
(afterwards Sir J. P. Kay-Shuttleworth, Bart.) says that, as a
dispensary physician, he sometimes had to make his way to
the bedside of a patient suffering from typhus, by stepping
from one brick to another placed on the flagged floor, which
was covered with water some inches deep.   During the
prevalence of cholera, some bad cases were carried away in
canvas slings, on men's shoulders to the hospital, from
flooded cellars near Knott Mill.

In the year 1864, the general death-rate was unusually
high, the average annual mortality rising 1·6 per thousand ;
while in the cotton districts the rate fell one per thousand,
upon the average of the preceding three years : though it
must be admitted that the rate was still higher than the

average of the country generally, it being 28, against 25·8. This preservation from pestilence and death was a matter for great thankfulness to all concerned, and was largely due, under Providence, to the wise precautions taken by Boards of Guardians and Relief Committees, and their officials; and to the large means placed at their disposal by a generous public.

It is a well-known fact that the marriage rate is affected by times of prosperity and adversity, increasing in those, and diminishing in these. And the days of the Cotton Famine furnished further proof of this. The marriages in the cotton districts during four years were as follow :—1861, 19,155; 1862, 16,263; 1863, 18,233; 1864, 17,490. An average of eighteen hundred and twenty-six less on the succeeding three years than in 1861. Five thousand four hundred and seventy-nine fewer in the three years; or nearly eleven thousand persons kept single, who might otherwise have sought for wedded bliss in holy bonds; without calculating the normal increase of ordinary times.

Happily, the increase of immorality, which might under such circumstances have been anticipated, did not result; for which we are greatly indebted to the religious institutions of our county, and to the supervision in sewing classes, &c., by ladies of culture, refinement, and position, of the youthful female population ; and to the care taken to provide for the instruction and innocent recreation of the youth of both sexes.

Neither did crime increase. Various authorities declared in May and June, 1862, that, notwithstanding the pressure of distress in the principal Unions, crime had decreased ; and even to the end of 1864, the character of the population was sustained.

It would be useless to deny that there were cases of imposition upon the committees, especially in the earlier stage of their operations ; but these, as a rule, were speedily found out, and such precautions taken as prevented a repetition of the same ; and we believe that no benevolent fund was ever distributed with greater care, or with fewer instances of what was intended for the really necessitous, falling into the hands of impostors.

In the cotton district—" During the three years ending Lady Day, 1864, the Guardians expended in the relief of the poor, £1,937,928 ; and the Local Committees, £1,372,454 ; making a total of £3,310,382 ; whilst in 1861 the Guardians of the Poor spent only £313,135." In addition to the amount distributed by Committees during the three years, as has been already said, large sums were disbursed in private bounty, which, though they could not be tabulated, none the less swelled the stream of benevolence which freely flowed.

The Central Executive adjourned *sine die* in June, 1865, without calling together the General Committee. However a final business meeting of this committee was held December 4th of the same year, when it was announced that the distribution of relief through the Local Committees had wholly ceased, no grants having been made by the Central Executive since June last. And what was still more satisfactory, the number of paupers in receipt of parochial aid in the Unions of the district, was but seven hundred and thirty in excess of December, 1861, when the stoppage of mills was but commencing. More satisfactory evidence that the pauperisation of the people, which had been greatly feared as the result of a large distribution of relief, could scarcely have been afforded; nor could stronger proof be desired than the smallness of this residuum, of the independent character of the Lancashire operatives, and of the wisdom with which these large funds, placed at the disposal of the Relief Committees, had been administered.

At this final meeting of the General Committee, special votes of thanks were passed to the Chairman, the Earl of Derby; the Vice-Chairman, Sir J. Kay-Shuttleworth; and the Honorary Secretary, Mr. J. W. Maclure; and a sub-committee was appointed for the purpose of raising a substantial testimonial to the last-named gentleman, who, when the legality of remunerating him for his services from the general fund had been under consideration, declared that under no circumstances would he receive a single shilling from the funds subscribed by the general public. The Executive Committee had already initiated, and liberally subscribed too, the Testimonial Fund, which ultimately amounted, to the best of our recollection, to something over £6,000; handed to Mr. Maclure, not as payment for, but in acknowledgment of, his incalculable services in aid of the distressed, given without stint, and, in the words of Lord Derby, " unflagging, invaluable and unceasing."

The cotton operatives of Lancashire manifested their gratitude to the Lord Mayor and citizens of London, for the munificence of their bounty during the three years of the Cotton Famine, by subscribing for a memorial window to be placed in the London Guildhall, which was uncovered on the 15th July, 1868.

The large balance remaining in the hands of the Central Committee, after all distribution had ceased, was retained for a few years, and ultimately £130,000, or upwards, was handed to trustees, as "The Cotton District Convalescent Fund "; the benefit of which is still reaped by many a Lancashire sufferer.

III.

THE DARWEN COMMITTEE.

THE following is a list of the gentlemen comprising the Darwen Relief Committee, organized in 1862 :—

Chairman and Treasurer : Eccles Shorrock, Esq.

Vice-Chairman : Rev. Philip Graham.

Honorary Secretary : Mr. S. A. Nichols.

Committee :

Rev. Geo. Berry	Mr. Thos. Fish
Rev. W. H. Blamire	Mr. D. Graham
Rev. T. Davies	Mr. H. Green
Rev. J. Denny	Mr. Thos. Green
Rev. T. J. Gale	Mr. Edward Gregson
Rev. C. Greenway	Mr. Josiah Gregson
Rev. D. Herbert, M.A.	Mr. W. H. Gregson
Rev. E. C. Montriou, M.A.	Mr. F. Gregson
Rev. G. R. G. Pughe	Mr. Jno. Hayes
Rev. G. W. Reynolds	Mr. Chas. Kendall
Rev. G. Robinson	Mr. Thos. Kenyon
Rev. J. Smithies	Mr. J. T. Kenyon

Rev. J. H. Unwin

Rev. D. Vandenweghe

Mr. D. Ainsworth

Mr. R. S. Ashton

Mr. W. S. Ashton

Mr. W. T. Ashton

Mr. J. Baron

Mr. A. Bullough

Mr. J. Carlisle

Mr. E. Coote

Mr. R. Cross

Mr. J. B. Deakin

Mr. Jos. Eccles

Mr. G. H. Openshaw

Mr. E. Openshaw

Mr. Jos. Place

Mr. J. G. Potter

Mr. Walmsley Preston

Mr. W. B. Ranken

Mr. Jas. Shorrock

Mr. Chris. Shorrock

Mr. W. Snape

Mr. Nathl. Walsh

Mr. Jas. Wardley

Mr. B. Wood

1862.

SUBSCRIPTIONS AND CONTRIBUTIONS TO THE DARWEN RELIEF FUND.

	£	s.	d.
Messrs. Eccles Shorrock & Co.	1000	0	0
Wm. Duckworth, Esq..:...........................	200	0	0
Do. For Christmas Dinners..	100	0	0
Do. For Overlookers' Fund..	50	0	0
Carried forward £1350		0	0

	£	s.	d.
Brought forward	1350	0	0
Mr. J. G. Potter	330	0	0
Rev. P. Graham ....,.....	220	0	0
Mr. Nathaniel Walsh	125	0	0
W. B. Ranken, Esq..................................	100	0	0
Messrs. Graham & Green...........................	100	0	0
Messrs. J. & J. Place	100	0	0
Messrs. J. L. & J. Gregson	100	0	0
Jas. Hodgson, Esq.	52	10	0
Messrs. C. Shorrock, Sons, & Waterhouse (Manchester).....................................	50	0	0
Messrs. J. & J. Eccles	50	0	0
Messrs. J. T. Kenyon & Co.	50	0	0
Messrs. W. Snape & Co.	50	0	0
Messrs. Heron, Baron & Edelston	50	0	0
Messrs. T. Fish & Son.............................	50	0	0
Messrs. E. Gregson & Son	50	0	0
Messrs. Shorrock & Dimmock.....................	50	0	0
Messrs. Nichols & Ashton	50	0	0
Messrs. Pickups & Halliwell	50	0	0
Messrs. Wardley Bros.	50	0	0
Carried forward £3027	10	0	

	£	s.	d.
Brought forward	3027	10	0
Mr. J. Carlisle	50	0	0
Mr. D. Graham.........................	50	0	0
Mr. W. Preston.........................	50	0	0
Mr. Jno. Walmsley	50	0	0
Mr. R. Leach	50	0	0
Mr. D. Ainsworth.....................	50	0	0
Mr. G. H. Openshaw	50	0	0
Mr. T. Gillibrand	50	0	0
Mr. Jas. Garstang.....................	50	0	0
Mr. E. Walsh	50	0	0
Mr. A. Bullough	50	0	0
— Silkenstadt, Esq.	50	0	0
— Schulz, Esq.........................	50	0	0
James Greenway, Esq.	50	0	0
Messrs. Ibbotson & Langford	50	0	0
Messrs. J. & R. Shorrock...........................	30	0	0
E. Hilton, Esq.........................	25	0	0
Mr. Jos. Greenwood.................	20	0	0
Messrs. Wood & Almond	20	0	0
Mr. W. Pickup.........................	20	0	0
Carried forward	£3892	10	0

	£	s.	d.
Brought forward.....................	3892	10	0
Anonymous, per Mr. Ranken	20	0	0
Independent Church and Sunday School at Uttoxeter, per Mr. Nichols	24	0	0
Mrs. Mason (Sydenham)	10	10	0
Mr. Thos. Grime	10	10	0
Mr. Livesey, jun.	10	10	0
Mrs. Carlisle..	10	0	0
Mr. & Mrs. Isherwood..............................	10	0	0
Rev. D. Herbert	10	0	0
Mr. Jno. Pickup	10	0	0
Mr. Singleton	10	0	0
Mr. Geo. Martin	10	0	0
Mr. W. Kay	10	0	0
Rev. C. Greenway	10	0	0
Mr. J. G. Holden....................................	10	0	0
Mr. Jas. Huntington, per Mr. D. Graham	10	0	0
Miss Hilton	10	0	0
Miss Imery	10	0	0
Rev. Jos. Hindle	10	0	0
Mr. Ralph Entwisle	10	0	0
Carried forward £4108		0	0

	£	s.	d.
Brought forward...................	4108	0	0
Mr. Richard Entwistle...........................	10	0	0
Mr. Chas. Kendall	10	0	0
Mr. D. Thwaites (Blackburn)	10	0	0
Stretton Church Choral Society, per Rev. P. Graham..	9	5	2
Mrs. E. Gregson	5	0	0
Mrs. W. H. Gregson	5	0	0
Rev. T. Davies.....................................	5	0	0
Mr. Robt. S. Entwisle	5	0	0
Mr. Jno. Gregory	5	0	0
Mr. R. Robinson	5	0	0
Mr. Hy. Watson	5	0	0
Messrs. H. T. & R. Timperley	5	0	0
Messrs. Simpson & Son (Preston)	5	0	0
Mr. Jas. Salmon	5	0	0
Mr. Jno. Taylor	5	0	0
Mr. Jno. Leach.....................................	5	0	0
Mr. L. Harwood	5	0	0
Mr. L. Roberts......................................	5	0	0
Mr. E. Gregson.....................................	5	0	0
Carried forward £4222	4222	5	2

	£	s.	d.
Brought forward............	4222	5	2
Mr. Jno. Dearden....................................	5	o	o
Mr. Wm. Thornber	5	o	o
Mrs. George Shorrock	5	o	o
Mr. E. Gregson	5	o	o
Mr. T. Pickersgill	5	o	o
Rev. E. C. Montriou	5	o	o
Miss G. H. Cunliffe................................	5	o	o
Mrs. Hy. Carlisle (London).......................	5	o	o
Mr. Atkin (Liverpool)	5	o	o
Mr. Macnama (New York)	5	o	o
Small sums, under £1............................	5	12	7
Mr. Jos. Bentley	4	o	o
Mr. A. Elliot (Windsor)	3	3	o
Messrs. Langton & Bicknell (London)	3	o	o
Mr. Singleton's Boys	2	10	o
Mr. H. Beesley	2	10	o
Mr. Jos. Nall	2	2	o
Mr. Cocker	2	o	o
Mr. Jos. Chadwick	2	o	o
Messrs. Parker Bros................................	2	o	o
Carried forward £4301	2	9	

	£	s.	d.
Brought forward	4301	2	9
A Friend	2	0	0
A Lady, per Rev. J. Edouard (Leominster) ...	2	0	0
Mr. Vaughan	2	0	0
Rev. G. W. Reynolds	1	1	0
Rev. J. H. Unwin	1	1	0
Mr. Jno. Thompson	1	1	0
Mr. J. Riley	1	1	0
Mr. H. E. Poole	1	0	0
Mr. A. Aspinall	1	0	0
Mr. Andrew Kay	1	0	0
Mr. Thos. Kay	1	0	0
Mrs. Burgess	1	0	0
Mr. Jno. Wardley	1	0	0
Mr. J. Almond	1	0	0
Mr. N. Holden	1	0	0
Mr. J. Earle	1	0	0
Mrs. Bayne	1	0	0
Miss Bayne	1	0	0
Mr. Harper (Twelve Trees, London)	1	0	0
Two Young Ladies at School—work sold	0	12	0

Carried forward £4323 18 9

	£	s.	d.
Brought forward......	4323	18	9
Collected by Miss C. Smalley at New Inn......	3	1	4
Do. by Freemasons at Mr. J. Bentley's...	1	10	0
At Messrs. Potter & Co.'s Belgrave Works......	6	12	7
Do. Hollins Works	9	10	10
At Messrs. W. Snape & Co.'s, Livesey Fold ...	12	9	8
Mr. Jno. Knowles's Men, working at India Mill	3	9	0
From the Mansion House Fund..................	875	0	0
Do. for Xmas Dinners	66	0	0
From the Central Committee	700	0	0
From Australian Educational Fund, per Central Committee	180	10	0
	£6182	2	2

CONTRIBUTIONS IN KIND.

Mrs. Jno. Isherwood, £5 worth Clothing Materials.

Hy. Mason, Esq. (Sydenham), 1 package Clothes.

Miss Nichols (Weymouth), per the Secretary, 2 bales Clothing.

Mrs. S. Heron, 1 parcel Flannel for the Sewing Classes.

Mansion House Committee, 4 packages Clothing.

Religious Tract Society (London), £5, Library for the Schools.

Society of Friends' Relief Committee, 15 barrels Flour.

Central Committee, 1 barrel Beef.

1 package Venison.

9 packages Bacon.

4 packages Bread.

2 hampers and ⎱ Wine.
½ doz. bottles ⎰

186 barrels Flour (of which 80 barrels *ex* the " George Griswold ").

6 packages Clothing.

25 suits of Clothes, for Workers on the Footpaths.

The Population of Darwen from the beginning of the century to that of the present decade, according to the census returns, has been :—

1801	1811	1821	1831	1841	1851	1861
3,587	4,411	6,711	6,972	9,348	11,702	16,492

1871	1881	1891
21,278	27,589	34,192

The writer first saw a cotton factory in the early evening of a day in May, 1829, when from the top of a coach rolling down Bull Hill, the lights through the windows of Bowling Green Mill opened upon him, a very small child, a fairy vision which he has never forgotten.

What had once been the factory of Mr. James Grime was we believe, converted into cottages, and others built after the destruction of his dandy looms by the rioters in 1826, with the money paid by the County as damages, and Bowling Green Mill was, in 1829, the only one in Darwen; and then belonged to Messrs. Carr & Co., being purchased from them the following year by the first Mr. Eccles Shorrock, an unfamiliar name at the time, but soon to become a power in Darwen, as that of a man who gave the chief stimulus to the cotton trade there.

At Earnsdale, in the house of Mr. Alfred Potter, a rather harum-scarum but most kind hearted gentleman, the writer and a younger brother visited, and their parents were the guests of Messrs. Eccles, of Lower Darwen, while their own home, Chapel Cottage, was being prepared for residence. The Eccles family then consisted of six brothers and three sisters. The sisters, the eldest of whom was the Lady Bountiful of her neighbour-hood, all passed away many long years ago. Of the brothers, the elder three had arrived at man's estate, while the youngest was a child. All lived together in the family house adjoining the mills started by their father a full century ago, and none of the workpeople of that firm, to the best of our recollection and belief, ever stood in need of

extraneous help, but were looked after and cared for by their
masters.   The brothers too have all gone, the last being he
who was Chairman for so many years of the Board of
Guardians of the Blackburn Union, and was ever held in
the highest esteem, for his straightforwardness, integrity and
worth.

It is a very rare, if not unique, circumstance, that the
works at Lower Darwen, of which the buildings erected a
hundred years ago still form a part, are at the present day
run by the grandson of the original founder, who is yet a
comparatively young man.

The Potters, and the Eccles family of those days, were all
staunch Nonconformists, and worshipped at the old sanctuary
on the hill, Lower Chapel.

The sexton and one of the deacons there, was John
Shorrock, of Chapels, as original a character as any notability
of Darwen.   His repertory of racy, side-splitting stories was
in request at many a " stir," and worthy of frequent repetition.   If he did not boast of the fact he had certainly no
desire to conceal it, that when he married, the sole possession
of his bride and self was one half-crown.   Yet with their
hand-looms, in the days when the loom-shops rang with sweet
music from many a household choir, he brought up respec-
tably a family of sons and daughters ; though we believe his

descendants are not numerous in Darwen. His connection with these pages is, that he was the uncle and great uncle of members of the Relief Committee, and bore the same relationship to other contributors to its fund.

In 1861 the Township of Over Darwen (as Darwen was then called) had a population of 16,492 ; and its ratable value was £33,260 15s. In 1891 the population was 34,192, and ratable value £104,954.

In 1862 it contained thirty-three cotton mills, two print works and eight collieries, and the number of people employed in these, and other works of the town, was 8,078.

It was not till the autumn of this year that distress from the Cotton Famine began to be felt at Darwen, though prior to that time much suffering prevailed in other parts of Lancashire. The present writer, staying at Blackpool with his family in the early autumn, felt much compunction, and distress of mind, that he could not tell how he might take an active part in the relief of the destitution that was fast becoming prevalent throughout the county, and which threatened to become intense as winter approached ; and well remembers his relief at the receipt of an invitation among his letters one morning, to become the Secretary of a Relief Committee which it was proposed to form for Darwen. He gladly acquiesced, and on returning home,

after consultation with the leading men of the town, who
had suggested the movement, convened a meeting, which
was held in the Board Room, at Peel Baths, on Monday,
September 15th, " To take into consideration the state of the
town, and the best means of relieving the distress." The
meeting comprised most of the clergy and ministers, with
the principal employers of labour.   The chairman and
secretary were appointed, and after some discussion it was
resolved, that a committee be formed " to inquire into the
amount of distress in the township, and the best means of
affording relief." A list of subscriptions, about two thousand
pounds, was announced, the General Committee formed (the
list has been already given, some of the names of which
were added subsequently) and a sub-committee appointed to
divide the town into districts, with a view to the requisite
inquiries.

The sub-committee met on the evening of the same day ;
and the Rev. Philip Graham was chosen as its chairman.
The town was divided into fourteen districts, (the work in
some of which proved so onerous that they had afterwards to
be sub-divided, and more visitors appointed), each of which
was undertaken by two gentlemen, who consented to
conduct the inquiry ; and the meeting was adjourned till the
following Saturday, September 20th.

At the appointed day the sub-committee reported, that "generally speaking, the amount of distress is not yet very great, although there are many who need immediate relief; and that it is desirable that a Relief Committee should at once be formed, and some regular organization established."

The General Committee had adjourned for a week, and re-assembled on the 22nd September—when this report was presented. The committee resolved itself "a permanent one, to meet every Monday;" appointed the twenty-eight visitors, with several other members, a Relief Committee to take measures for the immediate relief of the necessitous cases reported, and to organize a system of distributing relief in the township. Considerable discussion took place as to the scale of relief, and it was ultimately decided that such an amount should be given, as would make up a total income of one shilling and ninepence per head. And now the work began in earnest; that of the visitors was not confined to the discovery of cases needing relief and administering it; their duty was also to find out who in their districts could subscribe to the funds of the committee, or aid in the distribution. They were to apply at all mills and other places of employment at full work, and ask the artisans and operatives thereat employed, to make weekly contributions to the Relief Fund. They were soon directed to wait upon

the mill-owners, and request them to provide for the continued attendance of all half-timers at school; and also to
see that the children and young people of all families
relieved, were constant in their attendance at school, the
committee promising, where necessary, to pay the fees.

Another very important duty of the visitors was to take
precautions against acts of imposition, which were tried here
as elsewhere. Some of the visitors were very soft-hearted,
and lent a ready, and often credulous, ear to every tale of
woe. Two clerical gentlemen especially, brought harrowing
tales, which might have melted hearts of stone, time after
time, to the committee, of cases in their districts. But when
these cases were sifted, they not infrequently proved very
different to what had been represented. The late Mr. J. T.
Kenyon was invaluable to the committee in such cases. He
seemed to know almost every one in Darwen, and when he
touched with his Ithuriel spear the bubbles floated by the
compassionate pleaders, the labours of the committee were
lightened by the amusement afforded in contrasting the
two pictures presented. It was soon found necessary to ask
Mr. Kenyon to act as Honorary Visiting Secretary, in which
capacity he rendered true service; going to every part of the
town where special inquiry was needed, and taking no rest
till he had thoroughly sifted every statement. He was

indefatigable in the work, and though determined to brook
no deception, was too tender-hearted to let any really
necessitous human being suffer, but would rather have given
the help himself, than the needy should go empty away. He
is no longer with us, and we are glad to pay this tribute to
his memory.

Notwithstanding the vigilance of the committee, several
cases of imposition, and of obtaining relief tickets by false
representations were discovered, most of which were passed
over on the guilty parties signing a confession, and refunding
the money; but it was thought necessary to prosecute one
woman, who was tried at Preston, pleaded guilty, and
sentenced to three months' imprisonment. Relief was rarely
given in money, the rule being in kind, and the following
was the form of tickets distributed by the committee and its
visitors :—

" Supply   with provisions to the amount of
                  and enter on the back of this ticket what you
supply, with the price of each article."

These tickets were taken by the recipients to any trades-
man they chose; thus giving the opportunity of some slight
assistance to the shopkeepers of the town, many of whom
were suffering not only from lack of trade, but from non-pay-
ment of debts in their books. All tickets for provisions,

clogs, òr coals as afterwards distributed, were sent in at the
end of each month to the Secretary, who certified their
correctness, and gave the holder an order upon the Treasurer
for payment.

The Relief Sub-committee at an early sitting, after considerable discussion decided, that "as a rule" the relief
administered should be supplemental to that afforded by the
Board of Guardians; and a deputation was appointed to
wait upon the Board, and request the Guardians to be liberal
in the relief granted to applicants from this district. The
Guardians were also requested to supply the Secretary with
a weekly list of those obtaining relief, and the amount given
them, as a check upon the statements of applicants to the
committee. At the next meeting the deputation reported
that the Guardians "had received them cordially, and
acceded cheerfully to their requests." Mr. Thomas Kenyon,
as a Guardian, was elected a member of the committee.

The committee asked the Co-operative Society to favour
them with a list of shareholders; and on refusal instructed
the Secretary, in order to prevent collision with the Society,
to ask for a list to be used by himself privately, as a precaution against mposition, and not that the committee wished
to interfere in any way with the members of the Society, or
to compel any of them to part with such shares as were

requisite to retain their interest therein. The directors still refused, and we do not dispute their right in their discretion so to do.

The town was placarded with a list of the districts into which it was divided, and the names of visitors attached to each district, to whom those requiring aid might apply.

The General Committee and the Sub-committee now met weekly, that on the Monday, this on the Wednesday; and the latter was usally occupied for many hours in scrutinising the numerous cases presented by the visitors, who were expected to give full particulars of the state of all families requiring aid in their respective districts.

The committee soon found that other relief than food only, was needed; and exactly a month after its formation resolved that: "Experience has already convinced us that the Relief Committee should take measures for supplying poor people with articles of clothing and bedding—that the sum of £100 be appropriated in four instalments for this purpose . . . and that the first £25 be expended at once in wearing apparel by the Secretary." "That the distribution of these articles be made upon the same principle as that upon which the tickets for relief are already given out. That every article be stamped as 'Lent by the Darwen Relief Committee.'" This was an act of precaution against

such articles finding their way to the pawnshop, and not that
it was intended ever to demand their return from the
recipients.   The £100 soon swelled into £400—and when
this had been spent another £200 was so appropriated.

After another short interval it was found that a supply of
clogs was needed, and it was decided to get them if they
could be obtained on the same terms as those given by the
Guardians.   The cloggers of the town were interviewed,
and an arrangement made that clogs should be supplied by
them, on order by tickets.   Circulars were next addressed
to the drapers, asking for stocks of clothing materials suitable
for distribution.   The Clothing Committee which had been
appointed—Messrs. Graham, Herbert, and Nichols—visited
their shops, and made acceptable clearances of many shelves.

At the beginning of December, coals were found to be
needed by many who had not the wherewithal to procure
them.   So a Coal Committee was appointed, to whose use
money was set apart ; and not a house in Darwen was longer
without fuel, though not many such fires were to be seen in
the cottages during that winter, as the large ones of which
the Darren house-wives are unquestionably so fond.

The committee found the question of rent a perplexing and
difficult one.   The weekly relief granted was for food only.
At an early meeting it had been proposed, " That in every case

the net amount of income after rent is deducted, shall be the amount with which this committee deals"; but an amendment was carried, "That in every case where the visitors find a difficulty in the way of rent, they recommend the applicant for relief to ask the landlord to forego the rent for the present; and, on refusal, the visitors bring the case as a special one before the committee."

At Darwen, as elsewhere, were some landlords who, while they might be able to wait for, or even to lose, their rents, were unwilling to do so; and there were many more who were quite willing to wait, but could not afford—and yet they could not get payment from their tenants. The committee could not undertake to pay rents, and in November, on the motion of the Secretary, the committee resolved— "That the question of rent having been found by the committee a very difficult one with which to deal, the (foregoing) resolution . . . . be rescinded; and that, in future, rents form no ground of consideration with the committee, but that the amount of relief be henceforth raised, and incomes from all sources fixed, at the following scale : for one person, two shillings and sixpence; families of two persons, two and fourpence each; three persons, two and twopence each; four persons, two shillings each; five persons, one and tenpence each; six persons and upwards, one and ninepence each; and that an extra allowance shall be made for such members of families as are at work."

At an early meeting, in October, two of the clergy moved, "That the Relief Committee extend its operations to the ecclesiastical boundaries of the two Over Darwen parishes, and that subscriptions be asked from landowners resident therein"; but an amendment was carried, that the committee confine its operations to the township of Over Darwen, but give favourable consideration to any cases of distress over the boundaries, if the applicants have worked habitually in Darwen. It was afterwards however resolved, that the townships of Eccleshill, and of Yate and Pickup Bank, be included in the operations of the committee; and that Eccleshill be divided between two of the existing districts; Yate and Pickup Bank being constituted a new district, with the Revs. G. W. Reynolds, of Hoddlesden, and J. H. Unwin, of Belthorn, as visitors.

It has been already stated that the committee had offered to pay children's school fees when necessary. For the first month they had to pay but for sixty children; at the end of the second month the number was increased to four hundred and thirty. It was also proposed that night-school fees be paid for persons in need of relief. This was referred to the School Committee, who after much deliberation decided, that as the question involved complications, they cannot recommend its entertainment by the committee. They were in less hesitation at coming to this conclusion, because that in the meantime, offers of private assistance had been generously made.

On the 20th October, the committee requested the Chairman and Secretary to communicate with the ladies of the town, with a view to their undertaking the formation and management of Sewing Classes; and that the ladies be informed that it is the wish of the Relief Committee, that the classes work not less than five days in the week; that a paid superintendent be employed; and that instruction in reading and writing be combined with that of sewing. It was resolved, "That no girl be admitted into the Sewing Classes under the age of fifteen; and that anyone now at school be not allowed to change without permission from this committee." Also, "That twopence for every day's attendance, in addition to the ordinary relief ticket, be allowed to the members of the Sewing Classes; and, if the attendance be confined to five days a week, the allowance for the five days be a shilling."

The Mechanics' Institution at that time occupied the suite of rooms over the old Market House, now tenanted by the Liberal Club. The Council of the Institute offered the use

of the assembly and class rooms to the committee, for sewing and other classes which might be formed, and the offer
was gladly accepted.

The ladies were convened by circular, and, though the
day on which they met was most inclement, they assembled
to the number of forty—whose names we wish we could
give—formed a committee amongst themselves, and arranged
to meet, each at set times, to undertake the management of
the classes. They soon gathered eighty willing learners,
whose busy fingers plied the needle, and made garments
wherewith to clothe themselves and others. While some
of the ladies taught sewing in the large room, others gave
reading, writing, and cyphering lessons in the class-rooms.
They took great interest in their *protégées*, and very soon
asked the committee to have backs put to the forms in the
assembly-room ; but the Secretary was instructed to reply,
" that it is the wish of the committee for the present to
avoid all unnecessary expense." They also addressed notes
to the visitors, asking garments for various members of the
classes, to which, as far as possible, they received a liberal
response. They wished the ministers of the town to attend
and open the meetings, but were recommended by the committee to do so themselves, with prayer or otherwise, as they
should think fit. They were empowered to make their own

arrangements with the superintendent and cutter-out of the sewing-classes, and to purchase the requisites for work, with the concurrence of the committee's Secretary.

It was soon found necessary to engage more paid help for the cutting-out, and the ladies were authorised to employ any number required, at the rate of a shilling per day. The materials were all to be cut up in the work-room, under the immediate supervision of the ladies. The sewers could not make up all the garments required; so that material, cut out and prepared, after being stamped was in many cases given out by the visitors, to be stitched together by wives and mothers, at their own homes.

A loan library, of the value of five pounds, had been gratuitously supplied by the Religious Tract Society, London; and the committee purchased a good stock of the Irish Society's reading books, and other school materials, for the purposes of instruction.

The Sewing Classes had not long been started, ere it was thought desirable also to commence a school for youths and adult males. The visitors had been requested to see that all unemployed young women, receiving relief, attended the Sewing Classes; and they were also to inquire, and report to the committee, the number of youths and men in each district out of work, for whom it may be desirable to devise schemes of instruction, and to find employment in return for relief afforded them. They reported at the next meeting of the committee, that they had found a considerable number of such men and youths; and the Revs. P. Graham, D. Herbert, E. C. Montriou, T. Davies, W. Blamire, with the Secretary, were appointed a sub-committee to make the necessary arrangements for the provision of day classes.

The Baptist Church had not long left the upper room of William Street School, for their new chapel in Bolton Road; and this room was kindly granted to the Committee for school uses by Messrs. Eccles Shorrock & Co.. Benches were already there, and some desks; others were borrowed, spare ones from the Mechanics' Institution.

The Secretary was instructed to apply to the Central Committee in Manchester, for a grant for all the classes formed, from the Australian Fund at their disposal for this purpose; which was at once conceded.

The School Committee decided that a paid teacher should be engaged; they advertised for one in the local papers, and wrote to the British and Foreign School Society for advice and assistance. The advice was given, the assistance promised but not received. One of the applicants for the mastership was invited to an interview with the committee, but found unsuitable. Several others followed with the like result ; the interview was unsatisfactory, the applicants were not sufficiently qualified, or answers to inquiries made were discouraging ; and, as time was progressing and the necessity urgent, on the report of the Secretary that a townsman, Mr. Thomas Harwood Marsden, was willing to undertake a share of the duties, the committee decided that a trial should be made of the two local candidates, Messrs. Marsden and E. Gibson, combinedly.

This was accordingly done, and the committee had no reason to regret the appointments. The two masters entered heartily into the work ; their teaching of the kind of pupils placed under them was satisfactory, and we have reason to believe that the instruction given was appreciated by at least some of those who received it. The Men's School was opened with a short form of prayer ; the members of the School Committee alternately paid a daily visit ; and members of the General Committee were asked to inspect it as frequently as possible. We have given this detail of the operations of the School Committee as a specimen of the thorough work of all the committees ; and do not hesitate to say that in no part of the cotton districts was the Relief Fund administered with greater care, zeal, and discrimination, and at the same time with a more earnest wish and determination that none requiring help should be denied it, or, indeed, should avoid receiving it, than it was by the Relief Committee of Darwen.

Instruction at the adult school was given on Saturday morning, as well as on the other days of the week. The room was kept open daily from 9 a.m. to 9 p.m. ; five hours for school instruction, and during the remaining time for reading and quiet recreation. Newspapers and periodicals, chess, draught, and solitaire boards were supplied ; and the only condition of entrance was the maintenance of orderly behaviour. Good fires were kept up, and the room well-lighted with gas ; so that it was usually well-filled in the winter evenings, and the object gained of keeping many out of the cold, wet streets—if from nothing worse. Some of the young men, operatives of the town, also formed private classes—a sort of Mutual Improvement Society—which was continued after the close of the relief work, and to them the spare articles from the school were given.

In February, the number in attendance at the adult schoo had greatly diminished. The committee dispensed with the services of the junior master, and the duties were under-taken by the senior, with the assistance of some of the pupils as monitors. During March the number largely increased again, the number running up to sixty ; the apparent reason being a desire to be set at work on the footpaths, to which the school had so far been the avenue. So many men wished for this work, that the General Committee found it necessary on the 6th April to pass a resolution, " That in future, no men be so employed, except such as are recommended by the visitors, and passed by the sub-committee." When this was put into force the attendance rapidly fell off, and by the month of May was so reduced that the committee came to the conclusion to close the school.

Attention to the state of the public footpaths, not kept in repair by the ordinary local authorities, was suggested by Mr. W. T. Ashton, who has always taken much interest in the by-ways of the neighbourhood ; and on his motion a sub-committee, consisting of himself with Mr. Openshaw and Mr. J. T. Kenyon, was appointed, to "inquire and report upon the desirability of employing the men relieved by the committee to repair" such footpaths. On the report of this committee, to whom Mr. C. Kendall was added, it was resolved that a portion of the fund should be applied to the repair of the footpaths ; and that the sub-committee make such arrangements with the Local Board of Health as might be found necessary. This was done ; the surveyor assisted in the work ; proper supervision was engaged ; and operations speedily advanced.

The footpath work soon became very popular with the

men ; all out of employment who could get admittance to it, did so; and in May, when the necessity for other kinds of relief was fast diminishing, the expenditure on footpaths alone, exceeded that of all other branches together. By the end of this month general outdoor work was more plentiful, and the committee arranged with the Board of Health, that the men still employed should be placed under their surveillance, and the sub-committee ceased its supervision. In June the barrows, spades, picks, rakes, hammers and roller, used by the men, were presented by the committee to the Local Board.

The total expenditure upon footpaths amounted to £749 15s. 2d., and much of the committee's excellent work in that direction still remains ; being the most permanent, visibly, of all its operations, and a memento to the present generation of its existence, as was the similar work done in 1825, at what was long remembered as the " dole time."

Near the close of 1862, Dr. Buchanan was sent from London by the Privy Council to visit the cotton district, and report upon its sanitary condition. At his suggestion the committee instituted an inquiry as to the necessity and practicability of providing, in anticipation, a temporary hospital for fever patients, should such an epidemic break out. A sub-committee consisting of five members (four of whom are now no more) and the Secretary was appointed, which held numerous meetings, and selected the Old Workhouse for the purpose, making terms with the tenant in possession. But on consulting the late Mr. Wraith, whose experience for many years as parish doctor aided his judgment, it was decided to postpone such a measure for the time being. The result proved the wisdom of so doing, the town was mercifully spared any such scourge, and the general health of the district was maintained over, rather than under the average.

At an early stage of the committee's proceedings, a special fund was set apart for the separate relief of overlookers, and their families out of work. Mr. Duckworth, Lord of the Manor, generously gave a special £50 to this fund. A small extra allowance was made to these men, and the whole distributed partly in money, and partly in kind.

There was a proposal on the 1st December that a soup kitchen be established, but the question was postponed, and ultimately the thing was found unnecessary.

Before the end of the year, 1862, some of the manufacturers had begun to re-start looms hitherto stopped, but with yarns spun from Surat cotton, entailing so much more work and trouble to weavers, that some of them preferred to be kept by the funds of the Relief Committee, scanty as their allowance

was, rather than return to the mill.   This had to be met by
a resolution of the committee—" That any manufacturer
whose looms are standing for want of weavers, shall apply to
the visitors of the district, or to the Visiting Secretary, who
shall immediately communicate with weavers in the receipt
of relief ;· and that in case of refusal to take the work .thus
offered, the relief of such weaver shall at once be stopped "
—after which the difficulty seems to have passed away.

At an early date the committee had been requested to
give their consideration to the redemption of necessary
articles of clothing, &c., and repeatedly did so, but found it
so full of difficulty that action was from time to time postponed.   However on the 1st December they resolved to
apply a portion of the fund to the redemption of pledged
articles, on condition that they received the committee's
stamp.   December 17th they sat for the redemption of
pledges, and granted £13 10s. 2d. to various visitors for
that purpose ; and for the same December 23rd, £15 2s. 8d.

Early in the committee's course, mis-statements in the
London *Times* and other papers had to be corrected ; and
December 1st the Secretary called the attention of the committee to a letter in the London *Star*, grossly over-stating
the amount of destitution in Darwen, and was requested to
ask the writer, Mr. Harper Twelvetrees, for an explanation,

before accepting the donation of one pound which he had sent. Shortly afterwards a letter appeared in the Blackburn *Times*, reflecting upon the treatment by the Darwen Committee of the people of Yate and Pickup Bank. The Rev. G. W. Reynolds was requested to answer it, and at the next meeting the Secretary was able to report that he had done so in a most satisfactory manner.

As Christmas approached it was felt desirable that some special help should be given to those who would otherwise be without the means of participating in the wonted festivities of the season—a privation which had not before befallen the dwellers in Darwen within the memory of that generation. The Lord Mayor of London and Mansion House Committee had already made an offer of eightpence for each individual in receipt of relief, for this purpose; and £66 was so received from them, giving an eightpenny dinner to about two thousand persons. Mr. Duckworth also generously sent £100 to be distributed at the rate of one shilling per head for a Christmas dinner, or otherwise disposed of as the committee might deem best. It was decided that this sum should be given to the visitors of the districts, £5 in each, and £5 to the Secretary, for a dinner at this rate to necessitous *non-recipients* of relief, of which application of his gift the donor highly approved; and indeed no class needed it more, or deserved it better. Many of such as there were known to be, the difficulty was often extreme to get at them.

Some would rather have died than their wants should be made known; and yet when they were discovered and helped, none were so grateful as they, or so long remembered the kindness shown. It was a source of the highest pleasure to each member of the committee to be of service to such as these; and many a blanket and other useful article, without the stamp of the committee upon it as in ordinary cases, was quietly handed to them. The doctors of the town were very useful in discovering such persons, especially Mr. Wraith. The writer well remembers one such case named privately by him, which had not been suspected. A widow, with a business, but that business gone almost to nothing through the universal stagnation; a quiet, gentle body, and in consumption too. Her wants received attention, wine and other delicacies were sent to her, and we believe that her frail life was prolonged, to her children's joy, for a few more years than it otherwise would have been. Doubtless the visitors, and other active workers, could give many such instances.

The adult and sewing classes were not forgotten at Christmas, in our record of which we cannot do better than quote from one of a series of letters contributed at the time by the present writer, to the weekly paper of a town in Staffordshire, which had contributed both to the Lancashire fund, and to Darwen.

The following is the extract : "Darwen, January 1st, "1863. . . . Public tea parties, general now throughout "the country, are a favourite institution in Lancashire—and "not least at Darwen. New Year's Day is here, as with our "friends in North Britain, a far more universal holiday than "even Christmas Day; and this very night, notwithstanding "bad times, several thousands will drink tea in the various "Sunday Schools of the district. The rooms are tastefully "decorated with evergreens and artificial flowers—some of "them, when the gas is lit, quite gorgeous—and are most "creditable to the taste of the amateur decorators, whose "willing fingers are employed hours and days in the "adornment, and who work none the less heartily that "approbation is their sole reward. It was thought then, "since all else are looking forward to this kind of enjoyment, "can nothing be done for those who wish for it, but have "not the means of its attainment? The matter was named "to the committee, and a sum proposed to be divided for "the purpose between the two schools, the Adult Male "School, and the Female Sewing Classes. . . . The

" proposal was hailed as a capital idea, and carrried with
" acclamation, and the men's party came off last night.
" There were about two hundred present—men, and the
" wives of those married—and the extent of their material
" enjoyment may be imagined from the fact, that when
" the bills came in to-day their amount was just three times
" that of the grant made, which, however, was for men alone.
" After tea a meeting was held under the presidency of the
" vice-chairman of the committee, supported by several of
" its members. The speeches of these gentlemen, appro-
" priate to the gathering, were interspersed with most excel-
" lent singing by a well-trained choir, and also with what
" formed not the least attractive part of the evening's enter-
" tainment—the tricks of a negro conjuror. This man of
" colour is a resident, and a factory operative when he can
" get work, but failing that just now he attends the adult
" school ; and on being asked to exhibit last night, and to
" explain his tricks, which are most expert, he readily com-
" plied, and gained deservedly much applause. The Sewing
" Class tea party is to take place next week. One of a
" similar character, but not under the auspices of the Relief
" Committee, was held last Monday night, when a Mother's
" Class, numbering about a hundred, which meets in one of
" the schools of the town, under the care of two ladies of

" different denominations, were, with their husbands, regaled
" with tea. After tea the room was thrown open to the public,
" and a series of scriptural views was exhibited by a magic
" lantern ; shown by Mr. Whitwell, of London, gratuitously,
" and proved so highly attractive that it is a moot point
" still which of the two parties, Monday or Wednesday night's,
" was the most popular."

The committee were released from the dilemma into
which the caterers for the men's tea party had put them by
over-expenditure, by the late Mr. Eccles Shorrock, who
kindly paid the difference. The place mentioned above is
Uttoxeter, a small and by no means wealthy country town,
of some four thousand inhabitants. The town itself contributed £144 11s. 4d. to the Central Fund, and the friends
of the Darwen Secretary, of the Congregational Church and
School, sent him a cheque for £24, for distribution ; and
he, wishing the fact to be recorded in their honour, placed
it at the disposal of the committee, who, at his request,
authorised its division amongst a few members of the committee, for private beneficence.

Statistical inquiries were instituted at various times during
the period of the committee's operations. The following is
the result of a canvass made at the end of December,
1862 :—

	Operatives Usually Employed.	Now Working Full Time.	Now Working Short Time.	Weekly Loss of Wages.
Cotton Mills	6297	3298	1674	£1850
Print Works	215	14	161	65
Paper Making and Staining Works	718	718	—	—
Foundries	180	75	—	120
Joiners and Builders	59	19	28	30
Collieries	494	193	167	184
Quarrymen & Labourers	115	37	—	107
	8078	4354	2030	£2356

This forms the basis of a report furnished to the Central Committee, at their request, at the end of the year, viz. :—

Number of operatives out of work in the district ...   1694

    Do.   working short time   1830

    Do.   working full time   4354

Ascertained loss of wages £2356

Number of persons relieved by the committee 1817*

* Taken on the average of the last four weeks.

Weekly expenditure of the Committee :

	£	s.	d.
Wages paid for repair of foot-paths	9	0	6
General relief	68	2	8*
Clothing	85	10	0*
Expenses—nil. Total...	£162	13	2

Amount received and promised up to this time from strictly local sources £4349 1 9

The same from general sources, including the Central and Mansion House Committees £1178 18 2

Balance in hand, less positive liabilities £784 0 0

* Taken on the average of the last four weeks.

Of the number of persons relieved, 1,038 were also receiving relief from the Guardians.

At the beginning of March, 1863, there were found to be 5,906 persons working full time, and 713 short time, leaving 1,459 still out of work to complete the total of 8,078 ; and the weekly loss of wages was still £1,983.

The highest number of persons relieved in any one week at Darwen, was in the first week of December, 1862 ; when the committee granted provision tickets to the value of £75 15s. 3d. to 494 families, 1,974 persons ; 1,136 of whom were also relieved by the Guardians. From this point, with some fluctuations, the number gradually dwindled until the first week of May, 1864, when it had dropped to 30 persons, at a cost of £1 4s. 6d. ; at which it remained till the second week of June, after which all relief was stopped.

The following is a statement of the expenditure for the month of March, 1863 :—

	£	s.	d.
Provisions	164	11	3
Clogs	30	5	4
Coals	120	13	7
Footpaths	142	10	2
Children's School-pence	19	4	10
Printing, Stationery, Adult School, & Sundries.	16	10	4
	£493	15	6

The number of men now employed on the footpaths was 113 ; and the number of children whose school-pence were paid in March, 568, as follows :—

Schools.	Children.	Amount.		
		£	s.	d.
Trinity Church Schools	140	3	17	10
Belgrave	106	3	16	8
Hoddlesden and Pickup Bank	97	2	18	6
Belthorn and Pickup Bank	36	1	2	4
Carried forward	379	£11	15	4

Schools.	Children.	Amount.
		£ s. d.
Brought forward	379	11 15 4
William Street	49	1 13 6
Culvert	46	2 13 8
St. William, Catholic	42	1 4 6
Holden Fold...........................	29	0 15 10
Hey Fold	12	0 14 8
Astley Street...........................	11	0 7 4
	568	£19 4 10

The rate paid, as fixed by the committee, was 2d. per child per week, and the apparent discrepancy in some of these accounts arises from the irregularity with which the bills were sent in.

There was an increase in the number of persons needing relief during March, and the cause was supposed to be a temporary cessation of work for the festivities on account of the marriage of the Prince of Wales. On that day Mr. Eccles Shorrock gave a banquet in the Assembly Room to the Relief Committee and other gentlemen of the town and neighbourhood ; with a display of fireworks from the roof of India Mill at night. ' On the same day all classes were feasted ; there was no destitute person in Darwen on that day certainly.

The last week of March was the twenty-sixth week of the operations of the committee, and the Secretary presented them with the following summary of total expenditure :—

	£	s.	d.
For Provisions	1124	8	3
Clothing, Bedding, and Clogs ...	1038	16	4
Cash Distributions	138	6	0
Footpaths	377	6	2
Coals................................	190	8	2
Children's School Pence	74	1	2
Printing, Stationery, and Adult School	74	4	1
Sewing Classes	39	2	9
Sundries and Advertisements ...	15	15	3
Estimated Liabilities	50	0	0
	£3122	8	2

An average expenditure of £120 per week, in addition to the distribution of clothing and provisions sent from a distance.

In April there was five weeks' distributions to provide for, and the month's payments amounted to £556 9s. 11d.

The balance in the Treasurer's hands, after deducting liabilities, was £400, and there still remained unpaid subscriptions £2059.

In May the expenditure was greatly reduced, and of it the footpaths now took 57 per cent. of the whole, as will be seen from the following statement :

	£	s.	d.
Provisions	42	12	3
Clogs	7	1	8
Coals	4	14	6
School-pence	16	1	6
Adult School and other Expenses	8	14	0
Footpaths	106	3	9
	£185	7	8

On the 2nd February the General Committee resolved that their future meetings should be monthly only ; and that in case of any special business requiring attention, the Relief Sub-committee consider and decide upon it at their weekly meeting ; discretionary power being given to the Secretary to dispose of unused school materials.

At the May meeting the General Committee resolved that the operations of the Relief Sub-committee be at once suspended, and that all cases requiring relief should be decided by the Chairman, Vice-chairman, Secretary, and Visiting Secretary (of these four the Secretary is now the sole survivor); and very soon after, the duty of distribution devolved upon the Secretary alone for the remainder of the term, with the help of Mr. T. Green, who was afterwards Assistant Overseer of Darwen.

In June the committee adjourned for three months, unless convened by the Secretary on special circumstances arising.

At the end of the year 1863, the Secretary reported that the expenditure of the committee to date amounted to £4,128 11s. 7d., and consists of the following items, viz. :—

	£	s.	d.
Provisions	1471	17	10
Clothing, &c	1103	16	8
Footpaths	749	15	2
Coals	312	8	2
Children's School-pence	173	6	10
Adult School, Sewing Classes, and all other expenses	179	0	11
Cash Distributions	138	6	0
	£4128	11	7

In December, 1863, the Secretary received from Mr. Alexander Redgrave, Chief Inspector of Factories, a letter asking "for official purposes accurate information upon the subject of the relief of distress," and to be furnished "with copies of any printed reports or other documents issued by your committee, . . . or any documents explanatory of the condition of your district during the present year." To this the Secretary replied, "that this committee has not published any reports or documents, nor is it likely to do so until the close of its labours. . . . The distress reached the highest point here in the first week of December, 1862, when the number of persons relieved was 1,974. In the first week of the present year it was 1,401, from which, with some variations, it decreased to 182 in the last week of June, at about which number it has since stood, and the committee hope if no adverse circumstances arise to be able to dissolve in the approaching spring. In the weaving department of the cotton trade here there is abundance of work to be had, and great dearth of operatives, including winders, warpers, and weavers, especially the latter, for want of whom hundreds of looms are idle. The amount raised for this Relief Fund is over £6,000, of which fully two-thirds consists of local subscriptions, and the balance of grants from the Mansion House and Central Committees."

The committee held quarterly meetings for another year, the last of such, in diminished numbers, being held on the 6th June, 1864, when there were present: The Rev. Philip Graham (in the chair), Revs. W. H. Blamire and George Berry; and Messrs, H. Green, G. H. Openshaw, D. Ainsworth, C. Kendall, Jos. Place, Robert Cross, and Nichols.   But a special meeting was held November 28th, 1864, for the purpose of considering how a sum contributed by the Central Committee in Manchester for the relief of Hoddlesden should be distributed; that part of the district being seriously affected by the entire closing of the mills there.   A sub-committee was appointed for the purpose of such distribution; and this was the last labour that the General Committee was called upon to perform.

At some committee meetings strangers from a distance attended, and watched the mode of administering relief adopted in Lancashire.   On one occasion Mrs. Gladstone was present most of the morning; and was the guest of the Rev. P. Graham, at Turncroft.

When the labours of the committee were at the highest point, and contributions in kind were flowing in, it was found necessary to engage some paid help.   Mrs. Gregson, of the Peel Baths, was appointed storekeeper; and Mr. Thomas Green, who had assisted the relieving officer, was engaged to help in the work of distribution. When at any time there are many claimants for bounty, some are sure to be disappointed, and are apt to give vent to their discontent in an outrageous manner. Soon after these appointments the Secretary reported to the Committee that Mrs. Gregson, the store-keeper, had appealed to him in great distress on account of various caluminous charges being circulated in the town against her, which charges he had investigated, and found utterly false. This testimony was corroborated by the Visiting Secretary and Mr. Snape; and the committee passed a resolution of deep regret that any unjust and unfounded charges had been brought against Mrs. Gregson, and expressed their entire confidence in her integrity.

At the meeting in June it was resolved, on the motion of the Secretary, that the subscriptions due from each contributor to the Relief Fund be ratably apportioned, and the Treasurer be requested to obtain from those who have not yet paid up their full share, the amount due. It was also resolved that Messrs. W. H. Gregson and Alexander Briggs be requested to audit the accounts. The writer knows not if these resolutions were carried out, but no Treasurer's account was ever presented to the committee, which indeed never met again (except for the special purpose already intimated;) and as on the 22nd September, 1862, it declared itself "a permanent committee," it still exists in the persons of its survivors.   They, alas ! are now few in number, the lay members being greatly diminished.

It will be seen that there were originally fifteen clerical, and thirty-seven lay members.   Of those there are now, to the best of our knowledge, ten survivors, and of these but thirteen ; one-third of the ministers, and two-thirds of the · laymen having been taken—another proof of the probability of the clerical life being longer than that of a laymàn.   A French statistician has recently written, that his researches show that the status of a Protestant pastor gives a greater prospect of longevity than that of any other calling.   And we are glad to know. that the worthy representative of the Catholic clergy on the committee, the Rev. Desirè Vandenweghe, is still tending his flock.

Thus the labours of the Darwen Relief Committee came. to an informal end.   The Secretary, in anticipation of a meeting for dissolution, prepared a full report of the proceedings from the commencement, which still lies in his desk, complete, save that the last sentence is yet unfinished, and for ever will be.   The meeting was never called, which he admits to be more his own fault than that of any other now surviving member.   All such superfluous nonsense as that of votes of thanks to those who had borne the burden and heat of the day was dispensed with, not being in the bond. Yet it may be well in the future, for those who call upon their fellows for special labour, to remember that though words are but air, and the labourer seeks no other than his chief reward, which he finds in the consciousness of having done what he could, still it cheers, and strengthens him for further effort when called upon, to know that he has the recognition and approval of his colleagues.

The committee, as readers will see at a glance through the names, consisted of gentlemen of various denominations, and on such a board, if anywhere, the principles of a true " Evangelical Alliance," an alliance for deeds of mercy and of love, were to be found. Catholic and Protestant, Church-man and Dissenter, met and worked heartily together in acts of beneficence; and work more harmonious—each zealous only for the good of all—we cannot conceive while men are mortal and liable to err. Nor was the union or friendship merely in committee work. Men meeting there who would not else have met, learnt to know and appreciate one another, which led to the manifestation of kindly feelings. A county magistrate, not a member of the committee, said one day to the writer, " I asked Mr. ——, the Catholic priest, the other night to supper, to .meet our two young curates. I thought they met often at the Relief Committee, and why should they not meet here? They came, and a right pleasant evening we had."

An old Lancashire divine once said that "gratitude is often expressed without being felt, but seldom felt without being expressed." The recipients of relief were not ungrateful for the aid afforded them, though with true Lancashire reticence—a contrast to the fawning volubility of some peoples—they rarely gave expression to it; yet occasionally the committee received a tribute of thanks. One has been preserved, a letter from a factory operative, concluding, " I feel thankful to every kind friend who helped us in the time of need. To your committee I owe a debt of special gratitude for the kind assistance sent to me and my family while on a sick-bed in which my life had been despaired of; but with thanks to the great Author of life and death I am gradually recovering, I hope for some wise end. Accept, kind friends, these few lines as the tribute of a heart that cannot express all it feels for your kind sympathies, and those of the nation in general." This is supplemented by sixty-four lines of doggrel verse, which the composer must have taken for poetry, as he considerately gave the committee permission to "publish this communication if you think fit."

And here we introduce a few stories of applicants for relief to a Board of Guardians which will be easily recognised by Darwen readers, from the racy pen of the late Edwin Waugh, who was special correspondent for the *Manchester Examiner and Times* at this eventful period.

"A clean, old, decrepit man presented himself at the Board. 'What's brought you here, Joseph?' asked the chairman. 'Why au've nought to do, nor nought to tak' to.' 'What's your daughter Ellen doing?' 'Hoo's eawt o' wark.' 'And what's your wife doing?' 'Hoo's bin bedfast aboon five year.' A ticket for relief being given, the man looked at it, and turned round, saying 'Couldn't yo let me be a sweeper i'th' streets i'stid?'"

"A clean old woman came up, with a snow-white night cap on her head. 'Well, Mary, what do you want?' 'Aw could like yo to gi' mo a bit o' summat, Mr. Eccles, for aw need it.' 'Well, but you've some lodgers, haven't you, Mary?' 'Yigh, aw've three.' 'Well, what do they pay you?' 'They payn mo nought. They'n no wark, an' one connot turn 'um eawt.' 'Well, but you live with your son, don't you?' 'Nay, he lives *wi' me*, an' he's eawt o' wark too. Aw could like yo to do a bit a summat for us. We'se hard put to't.'"

"Another old woman presented herself, with a threadbare shawl round her head. 'Well, Ann,' said the chairman, 'there's nobody but yourself and your John, is there?'

' Naw.' ' What age are you?' ' Aw'm seventy.' 'Seventy?'
' Aye, aw am.' ' Well, what age is your John?' ' Hee's
gooin' i' seventy-four.' ' Where is he, Ann?' ' Well, deawn
i'th' street yon, gettin' a lood o' coals in.' "

"The workpeople very commonly nickname their work-
shops. A girl being asked where she worked last, replied
' At th' Puff an' Dart.' ' And what made you leave?'
' Whaw, they were woven up.' One poor, pale fellow said
he ' had wortched a bit at Bang th' Nation till he was taken ill,
and then they had shopped his place.' Another when asked
where he had been working, replied ' At Se'nacre Bruck,
wheer th' wild monkey were catched ;' alluding to the cap-
ture of an ourang outang which had escaped from a menagerie."

There were amusing incidents in connection with the
work at Darwen as elsewhere, and that not infrequently with
some of the articles sent from a distance. The visitors were
somewhat at a loss to know what to do with venison, deers'
heads and other parts sent by a kind-hearted gentleman, their
clients being unused to such fare. Some articles of clothing
were rather of the grotesque order ; such articles as dancing-
pumps, top-boots, veils, opera-cloaks, crinolines, and parasols
being found amongst them. One of the members of the
committee, a young gentleman from the Eastern Counties, a
relation of the writer's, appeared before him one evening in

full hunting costume, a scarlet coat of the time of our grand-fathers (with collar containing cloth enough for half-a-score of the present day) corded breeches and embroidered vest; which had been sent with other things by his friends at home.

Lancashire characteristics were, of course, manifested by applicants for relief. One worthy old man from the hill-side —and that he was a worthy the writer, who knew him well, can testify—called one day, and asked if Samooel wur in; he had coom cos he wanted relief. Another person knocked at the front door of one of the principal manufacturers, and asked the servant " if 'thanel wife wur in ?" The maid, a girl from the South, wondered what the old dame meant, and looked her wonder too. Impatient, she repeats " Is 'thanel wife in ? Awm Mrs. Blank, and tell her aw want " so-and-so. Lancashire operatives display a sturdy brusqueness which often puzzles strangers, and is misunderstood by those unacquainted with their sterling qualities; nor can their best friends deny that a mixture of the *suaviter in modo* with the *fortiter in re* on their part, would often be an improvement.

When the distress in the cotton districts was entering its most acute stage in 1862, Lord Palmerston, then Prime Minister, got hold of a tale which was not substantiated, that a spinner holding cotton, instead of using it, had sent it to Liverpool by night, and sold it there "for the sake of profit." The late Earl of Malmesbury, in his "Memoirs of an Ex-Minister," records under date July 31st, 1862 : "Lord Palmerston stated in the House that the manufacturers had sold the cotton which they ought to have kept to work their mills, utterly unmindful of the starving people around them. Mr. Cobden was furious, and said that the assertion was but another instance of that habitual recklessness and incorrectness for which the Premier was remarkable."

We in Lancashire were so accustomed to his Lordship's reckless statements, that none took the trouble to correct him. But when Mr. Gladstone, then Chancellor of the Exchequer, repeated the story at Newcastle, of the cotton sent away by night, and placed men who did such things in the same category as landowners who shut up rights of way, or refuse to allow dissenting chapels to be built upon their estates, the present writer, seeing that none else took up the matter, ventured to expostulate with the right honourable gentleman ; and in due course received a reply ; with which, as the *litera scripta* as well as the spoken words of this great orator are always acceptable to Darwen readers, we close this compilation.

"Downing Street, October 14th, 1862.

"Sir,—I beg to acknowledge the receipt of your letter

" and to say nothing can more meet my wish than that the
" opinion which I ventured to express should be freely
" canvassed. I at once accede to the soundness of the
" general argument in favour of what used at one time to be
" prohibited under the name of forestalling and regrating.
" But some limits upon human action which law cannot
" properly place ought to be placed by the sentiments of the
" individual himself : and I adhere, for my own part, to the
" opinion that the particular mill-owner, if there were one,
" who in selling his cotton had to provide for sending it away
" by night, ought to have perceived in the necessity for his
" singular precaution, all circumstances considered, a clear
" proof of the impropriety of the action he was about to
" commit. I by no means presume however to deliver this
" opinion with any pretence to authority, glad as I should be
" to believe that the public mention of the subject was
" likely to have any influence in preventing a repetition of
" the act. Pray accept my thanks for the tone in which you
" have treated the matter, and allow me to remain, sir,

" Your very faithful servant,

" W. E. GLADSTONE.

" P.S.—I am glad to hear an account comparatively
" so favourable of the state of Over Darwen and of the
" exertions made there."

A LANCASHIRE DOXOLOGY.

"Some cotton has lately been imported into Farrington, where the mills have been closed for a considerable time. The people, who were previously in the deepest distress, went out to meet the cotton : the women wept over the bales and kissed them, and finally sang the doxology over them."—*Spectator* of May 14th, 1863.

"Praise God from whom all blessings flow."
Praise Him who sendeth joy and woe ;
The Lord who takes,—the Lord who gives,—
Oh ! praise Him, all that dies and lives.

He opens and He shuts His hand,
But why, we cannot understand ;
Pours and dries up His mercies' flood,
And yet is still All-perfect Good.

We fathom not the mighty plan,
The mystery of God and man ;
We women, when afflictions come,
We only suffer and are dumb.

And when, the tempest passing by,
He gleams out, sun-like, through the sky,
We look up, and through black clouds riven,
We recognise the smile of Heaven.

Ours is no wisdom of the wise,
We have no deep philosophies :
Child-like we take both kiss and rod,
For he who loveth knoweth God.

THE AUTHOR OF "JOHN HALIFAX GENTLEMAN."

1863.

50

Milton Keynes UK
Ingram Content Group UK Ltd.
UKHW020807111224
3599UKWH00002B/7

9 781020 654206